I0099199

Mary Wilson and her
Wild and Wonderful Family

Mary Wilson and her Wild and Wonderful Family
Copyright © 2025 – Pat Smith
Illustrations Copyright © 2025 Pat Smith
All Rights Reserved

No part of this publication may be reproduced in any form or stored, transmitted or recorded by any means without the written permission of the author.

Sharon Kizziah-Holmes – Publishing Coordinator

Published by Kids Book Press
An imprint of Paperback Press, LLC
Springfield, Missouri

ISBN 978-1-964559-65-0 (Paperback)
ISBN 978-1-964559-66-7 (Hardcover)

Dedication

Sharron Wilson Jackson, for sharing your mom's very special stories with children all over the country.

Thank you, Mrs. Bennett's Fifth Grade Class students for reading and critiquing Mary Wilson and her Wild and Wonderful Family.

Mary Wilson and her Wild and Wonderful Family

written by: **Pat Smith**

illustrated by: **Barbara Nuetzmann**

revealed by: **Sharron Wilson Jackson**

My name is Sharron. My mom's name is Mary Wilson. I'm going to tell you about our *Wild and Wonderful Family*

Where should we start my mom's story? I know, I'll tell you about the Baltimore Zoo! When mom was young it was not possible for an African American girl to be a zoo keeper! Girls were supposed to be moms or teachers or nurses – Not Zoo Keepers!

Mom would have to have super powers to be a keeper at the zoo!

As a young woman, Mom really wanted to take care of animals. She wrote letters every week to Mr. Watson, the Baltimore Zoo boss.

After a whole year of letters, Mr. Watson gives Mom a job! He says that she has a heart for animals, whatever that means.

Is it that Mom is not afraid of wild animals or is it that she is a hard worker? Is working hard a super power?

One day Sylvia arrives at the Baltimore Zoo. Mom is the zoo keeper in charge of gorillas and elephants, and Sylvia is a baby gorilla!

She had traveled for days and days in a small crate from Africa. She heard loud noises all around her.

Sylvia is only 3 months old and misses her mommy gorilla. She is the only baby gorilla at the zoo and the grown-up gorillas are too big and dangerous to be her friends.

Mom whispers to her, "It's ok, Sylvia, you're such a good girl. I love you. You're like a baby to me. Just a cute, tired, little, baby girl." But, Sylvia just kept on crying all day.

Later the zoo closed and stars came out, the nocturnal animals began making strange noises. Sylvia huddled in a corner of her cage.

The next night the zoo closed, but, Mom decided to take Sylvia to our house! We stopped at the corner grocery store and I carried Sylvia into the store wrapped in a blanket. A lady stopped and asked to see the baby so I pulled back the blanket.

What a surprise! The lady threw her food in the air and ran away. Sylvia happily munched on a banana saying "oowup oowup". I think that means, 'mmmmm good'.

Sylvia became my sister.

When Mom was a little girl, she had a cute cocker spaniel dog named Crackers. He loved saltine crackers, head snuggles and running to fetch sticks.

The zoo did not have dogs, but Mom discovered the joy of cats. They like snuggles, are playful and can purr. But, unlike cocker spaniels, zoo cats grow --- really BIG.

Bianca is a really big cat at the zoo, she is a Jaguar with beautiful spots. One day Bianca decided to play Hide and Seek on the main zoo pathway *outside* her cage.

Mom heard the call on her walkie talkie, "Mary! Mary! Bianca is out!"

Mom rushed to find Bianca and squirted her with water! Cats, even big ones, do not like water! Bianca ran back to her cage.

Bianca's my sister too.

Speaking of cats and sisters, I have another one!

She's the fastest animal on land. Do you know what she is? Laika is a Cheetah. She's the fastest runner in our family! Laika can run 70 miles per hour, as fast as a car! But, she sits still for Mom to brush her fur which makes her purr. Mom says, "It's like babysitting – only more so. She's family."

"Mom's job as zoo keeper also includes taking care of her animal kids. When Laika has a cold, mom gives her medicine. Laika doesn't like the medicine very much but, she loves my mom!

Laika is my speedy sister.

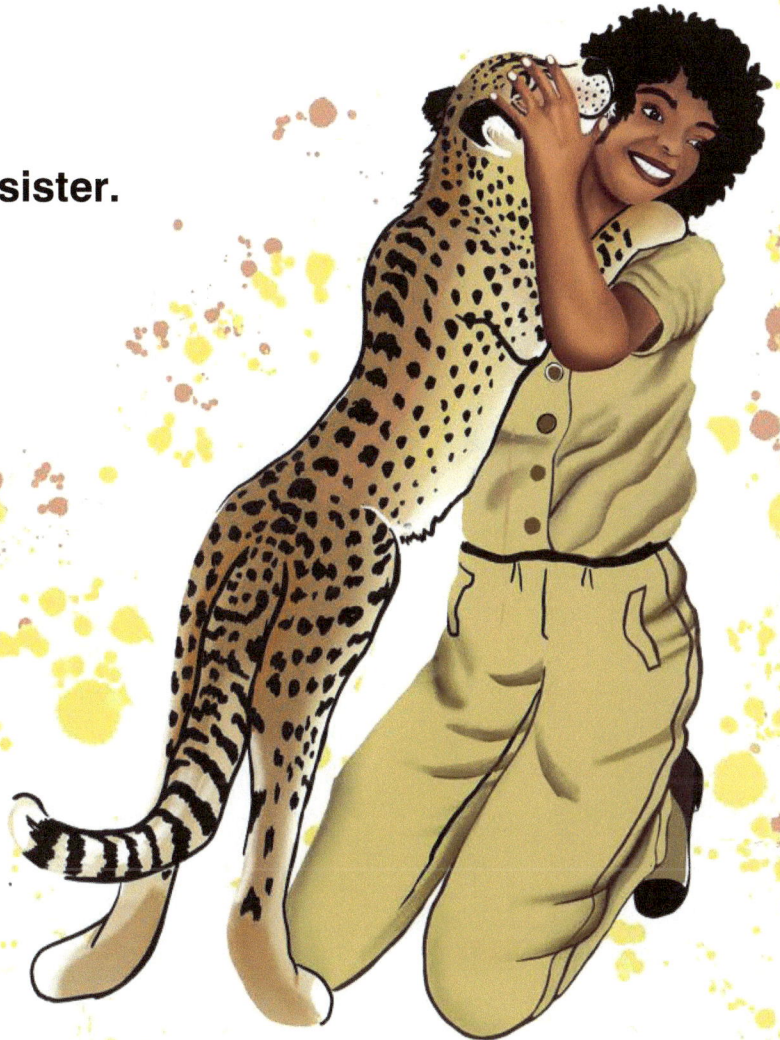

Many families have someone named Junior. We do too! Our Junior is a Kodiak bear with *big teeth* and *big claws*. He looks really mean. Lots of people at the zoo are super afraid of Junior.

Someone forgot to lock his cage door one day and Junior took a walk outside on the main pathway. Everyone ran!

Mary is not afraid of Junior and shouted at everyone, "Don't worry, Junior will follow me! I've got apples!"

The apples might have been magic because Junior followed Mom and her apples back to his home.

Junior is probably a cousin but since he's so BIG,
we call him Uncle Junior!

NETHERLANDS

NORTH SEA

•HOLLAND

GERMANY

BELGIUM

There's big news at the Baltimore Zoo today! A baby gorilla has been found in Holland, a country far, far away.

"We think he's a boy!" the keepers say. "There is a plan to buy him for Sylvia as a Valentine's Day present!"

I wonder, will Sylvia and the new baby boy gorilla be friends?

The new Gorilla is a boy! His name is Hercules! And, someone at the zoo has the grand idea that the two gorillas should get "married" on Valentine's Day! Maybe someday there will be more baby gorillas at the zoo!

The zoo invites all the newspapers to come watch Sylvia and Hercules getting married.

Hercules Arrives, Sylvia Is Cool

Valentine's Day comes and Mom puts a bridal veil on Sylvia's head, she's ready for the wedding.

But, where is Hercules?

FINALLY, after all the newspaper people leave, Hercules is delivered to the zoo. He leans in to give Sylvia a hug. Sadly, he's not very good at hugs and Sylvia jumps back. She does not like Hercules.

Hercules is my new brother.

Somehow Vaal, Mary's favorite Elephant, has escaped from the African exhibition and is strolling along the sidewalk.

Vaal is my onery sister.

"EMERGENCY! EMERGENCY!" the call went out on all the walkie talkies!
"Mary where are you? Vaal is out! Vaal is OUT!"

Mary answers, "Where! Where's Vaal? I'm on my way!

A zoo veterinarian runs toward Vaal pointing his tranquillizer gun at her shouting, "Everyone get back! Get Back!"

Mary shouts, "STOP! STOP! Do Not Shoot!"

"Vaal COME HERE! COME HERE! RIGHT NOW!"

"Vaal, you naughty girl! What were you thinking … taking off like that outside! You scared everybody! You come with me, right now!"

I don't think Vaal's hug for Mom is because of Mom's super power, I think Vaal loves Mom!

Twenty years after mom began her career as the gorilla and elephant keeper, Mr. Watson promoted her to Senior Zoo Keeper! Mary Wilson became the first African American female boss of the Baltimore Zoo.

I was about 10 years old when I asked Mom, "Do you think I could be a zoo keeper someday?"

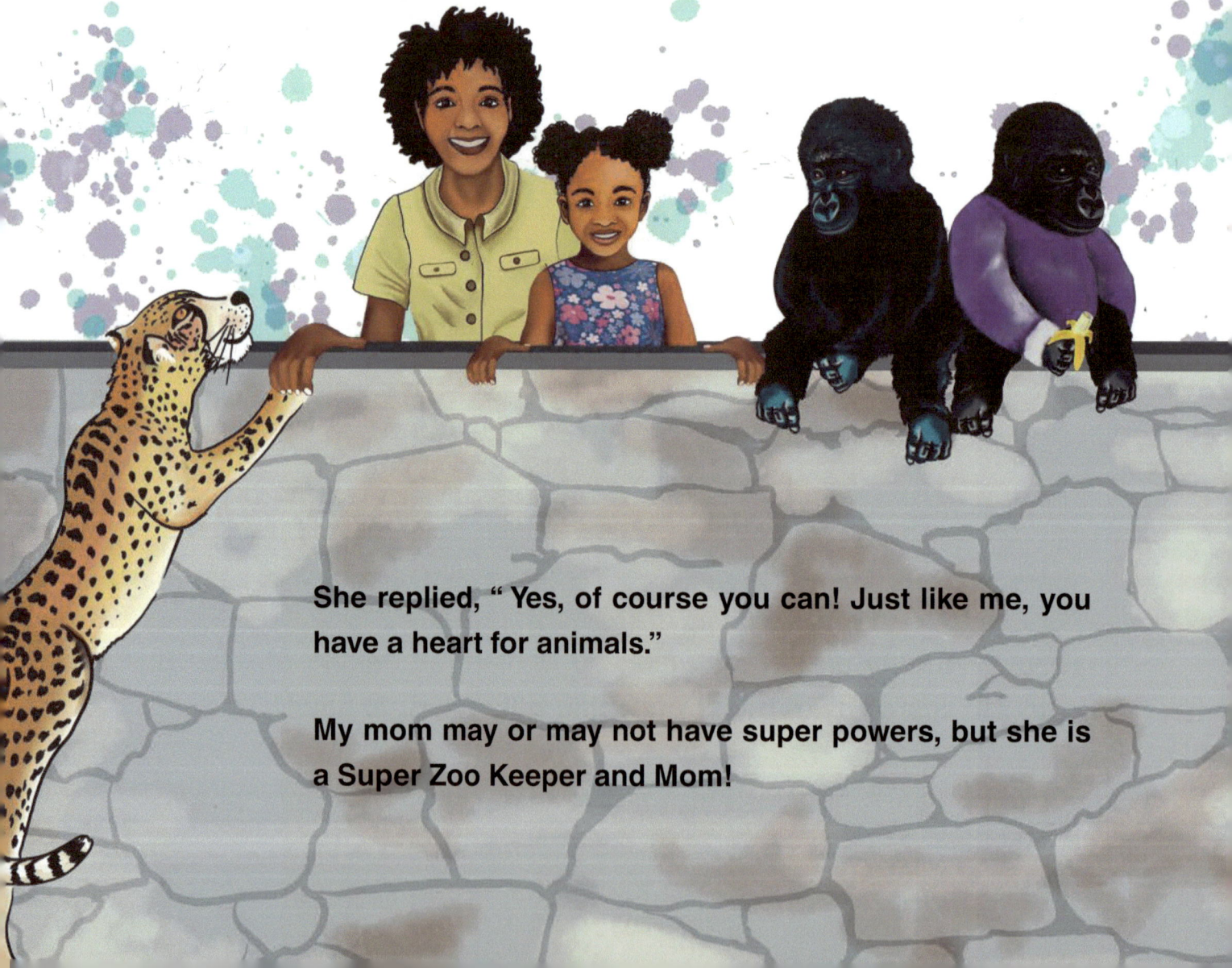

She replied, " Yes, of course you can! Just like me, you have a heart for animals."

My mom may or may not have super powers, but she is a Super Zoo Keeper and Mom!

Glossary

African Exhibition: A public area that showcases animals from Africa

Bridal Veil: A piece of net cloth that covers the head of a bride.

Cheetah: (chee-tuh) A fast, long-legged wild cat with a tan coat and black oval spots. Laika is pronounced - (Laykuh)

Elephant: An extremely large animal with a strong trunk and two long curved incisors (teeth).

Gorilla: A very large ape, usually black, from Africa that stands less erect than a chimpanzee.

Holland: A country across the Atlantic Ocean in northwestern Europe.

Jaguar: (jag-wahr) A large wild cat that has a tan coat with black spots that look like flowers.

Kodiak Bear: (ko-de-ak). A large brown bear that can grow as tall as 10 feet from Alaska and British Columbia.

Nocturnal animals: Nocturnal animals are playful and busy at night and sleep during the day..

Note from Sharron

Hi Everyone,

Mary Wilson is my mom. In 1963, she was the first African American woman in the U.S. to be employed as a zoo keeper at the Baltimore Zoo in Maryland where she worked for over 30 years.

It's a joy to share with you a few special moments from my mom's exciting career; I was really lucky to be with her for some of these adventures!

When I was young I didn't know how unusual or how important my mom's job was. After I figured that out, I knew that one day I would work with animals. Many years during summer break from elementary school I'd spend workdays with Mom. When other children went to summer camp, she'd take me to the children's area in the zoo. She first introduced me to all the barn animals and suggested that I treat each animal as family. Mom taught me what they ate and how to feed llamas, goats and cows. Her lessons I'll never forget.

In 1973, I became the first African American woman zookeeper at the Henry Doorly Zoo in Omaha Nebraska. Mom was a trailblazer for me, and all girls that love animals. Her story is an inspiration to anyone wanting a career working with wildlife.

I hope that you've enjoyed the true stories of how super brave my mom was. There is one animal species she was never fond of. Can you guess?

On behalf of my mom and me, we wish that you too, have the courage and persistence to follow your dream to whatever path you desire. Be bold, be kind, and stay focused. Sharron Wilson Jackson

PS: If you guessed a mouse, you are CORRECT!

Author's Note

I'd like to tell you how the true story of Mary Wilson came to fruition.

About a year ago, I met Jessica Cox and she and I decided to tell her unbelievable story. She has overcome great challenges to become who she was meant to be.

Born with no arms, everyone assumed Jessica would have limited abilities. However, today she is a licensed pilot, a golfer, she scuba dives, is a rock climber and more. Her achievements go on and on as her story continues.

But wait, I realized there are other great stories out there where people attained their goals despite their limitations. With Jessica's encouragement, I decided to tell some of these extraordinary stories.

In my opinion, Mary Wilson was the first African American female to become a Senior Zoo Keeper in the US and her story deserves to be told!

Thank you for letting us share it with you,

Pat Smith

Meet Mary Wilson

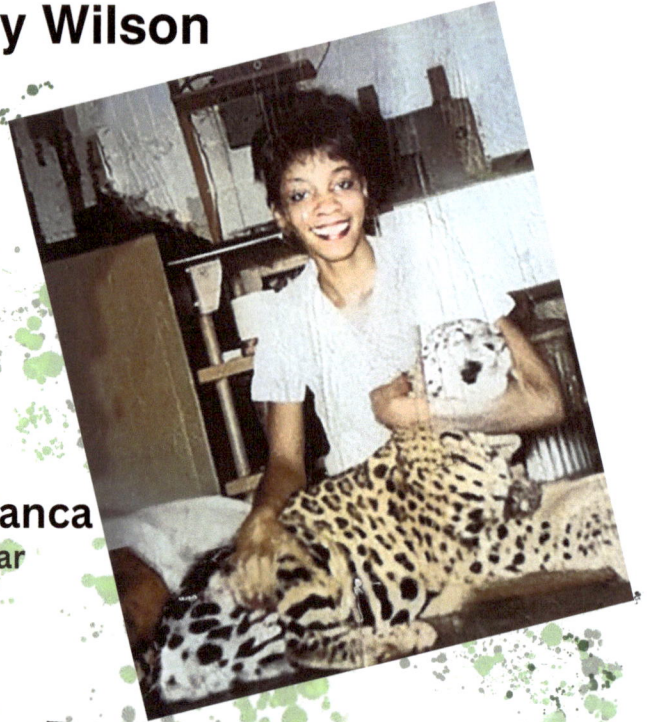

Mary & Bianca
the jaguar

Mary & Sylvia

Mary & Vaal

About the Author

Pat Smith

Pat Smith is a national award-winning educator. She twice received the Oklahoma Christa McAuliffe Fellowship, providing her with the resources to design an aerospace education program for elementary students in Broken Arrow, OK. The program included a mobile space shuttle lab that allowed students to become a 'astronauts' for the day, a space curriculum, teacher workshops and parent/community events. Pat was a U.S.A. Today All Star Teacher and is included in *Teachers*, a book recognizing 50 best educators from the U.S. and Canada.

After retiring from education, Pat researched the life of James Herman Banning, the first African American pilot to successfully fly coast-to-coast across the United States. As she dug through archives and interviews from the 1920's, Pat found that she had a great interest in searching out true stories of people who overcame great challenges in order to succeed. These stories have the ability to change the lives of children now and in the future.

About the Illustrator

From the moment Barbara Nuetzmann could hold a pencil, art has been a part of her life. A lifelong artist, she began drawing at a very young age and nurtured that early passion into a fulfilling career. She studied art at Oral Roberts University, where she developed her skills and deepened her love for creative expression.

Over the years, Barbara has shared her passion for art with students of all ages—teaching from 1st grade through 12th grade. Her favorite mediums include watercolor, charcoal, pencil, and photography. Whether capturing the delicate detail of a flower, the personality of an animal, or the likeness of a person, her work reflects a deep appreciation for the beauty in the world around her.

Barbara especially loves illustrating children's books, where stories come alive through her expressive and imaginative illustrations. Her work can be seen in Mary Wilson and Her Wild and Wonderful Family by Pat Smith, as well as several titles in the Melvin the Monarch series by Dorene Strebing.

Outside of the studio and classroom, Barbara finds joy in her family life. Married to her best friend for over 30 years, she is the proud mother of four amazing children and is continually blessed by her grandchildren, who inspire her every day.

Newspaper information courtesy of:

The Evening Sun (Baltimore, Maryland) Tues. July 2, 1963 . Page C1
The Evening Sun (Baltimore, Maryland) Jan. 6, 1965
The Evening Sun (Baltimore, Maryland) Jan. 15, 1966 Page 18
The Baltimore Sun (Baltimore, Maryland) Fri, Feb 18, 1966 · Page 44
The Baltimore Sun (Baltimore, Maryland) Tue, Apr 11, 1972 · Page 40
The Baltimore Sun (Baltimore, Maryland) Sat, Sep 5, 1981 · Page 11
The Baltimore Sun (Baltimore, Maryland) Tue, Aug 24, 1982 · Page 42

www.ingramcontent.com/pod-product-compliance
Lightning Source LLC
Chambersburg PA
CBHW041550040426
42447CB00002B/129